Once for all Delivered

ONCE FOR ALL DELIVERED

A Reformed, Amillennial Ordination Paper for
the Evangelical Free Church of America

benjamin vrbicek

Once for all Delivered: A Reformed, Amillennial Ordination Paper for
the Evangelical Free Church of America

© 2020 Benjamin Vrbicek

A publication of FAN AND FLAME Press in Harrisburg, PA

The Evangelical Free Church of America "Statement of Faith" and "discussion questions" in this book belong to the Evangelical Free Church of America and are used with permission.

Cover design: Dustin Tramel & Benjamin Vrbicek
Interior design: Benjamin Vrbicek

Paperback ISBN: 978-0997570274
Ebook ISBN: 978-0997570298

Special thanks to Rick Allen, Ben Bechtel, John Biegel, Paulo Freire, Noah Gwinn, and Stephen Morefield for reading and commenting on early drafts of my ordination paper. Thank you, Alexandra Richter, for your continued editorial assistance.

Scripture quotations are from The ESV® Bible (The Holy Bible, English Standard Version®), copyright © 2001 by Crossway, a publishing ministry of Good News Publishers. 2016 Text Edition. Used by permission. All rights reserved.

for Paulo Freire,
a pastor who serves well beyond his church

TABLE OF CONTENTS

PART III: PASTORAL AND PERSONAL SECTION

> *Marriage, Divorce, and Remarriage*
> *Abortion, Infanticide, and Euthanasia*
> *Role Distinctions in the Church of Men and Women*
> *Homosexual Belief and Conduct*
> *Theology of Worship*

> *Spiritual Disciplines*
> *Stewardship, Personal Finances, and Debt*
> *Sexual Purity*
> *Marriage and Family Priorities*
> *Social Drinking of Alcohol*
> *Accountability in Life and Ministry*

PREFACE

The week I completed my ordination was a week like no other I've had in ministry.

On Saturday I officiated a wedding.

On Sunday I launched our church sermon series in the book of Acts.

On Monday I crammed for my oral ordination exam by reading over my paper and most of *Evangelical Convictions*, a book published by the Evangelical Free Church of America to expound our statement of faith.

On Tuesday I underwent my four-hour oral exam, being asked and attempting to answer 154 questions (per the transcript) about theology and pastoral ministry. The rest of Tuesday and Wednesday, I enjoyed the Evangelical Free Church's Eastern District annual conference.

On Thursday I was subpoenaed to testify in court related to an appeal of a former church member currently in prison.

Finally, on Friday I had major reconstructive surgery on my right shoulder. With a tendon from a cadaver, a surgeon reconnected my pectorals major to my humerus bone by drilling three holes in my bone, laying the tendon across the holes, pushing the tendon through with grappling hooks, and sewing everything together. I'm not making this up. I wrote this preface with my right arm still in a sling, where it's been for two months.

When I started to put my children to bed on Tuesday night, the evening after my ordination, I collapsed on my own bed at 8 p.m. I thought I'd just rest for five minutes to steel myself for the job of putting our six children to bed. My wife had to finish the job, as I woke up from my five-minute nap ten hours later.

Again, it was a week like no other.

If you're reading this and considering the credentialing process in the Evangelical Free Church of America or any denomination, don't let my difficulties discourage you. It's a ton of work, but I learned so much in each stage of the process: the studying and researching, the writing and re-writing, the preparing for the oral exam, and finally being examined. The ordination process made me a more effective pastor, knocked off rough edges of my theology, deepened my sense of calling, and stirred fresh joy in God.

The Return of Christ

I'm told that my ordination is the first in the Evangelical Free Church of America (EFCA) for a candidate who holds to the amillennial view of the return of Christ. Our EFCA statement of faith formerly specified a "premillennial return of our Lord Jesus Christ" (Article 9, Christ's Return). Therefore, credentialed pastors in the EFCA formerly only took one of two views on the tribulation and millennium: either historic premillennialism or dispensationalism. In the summer of 2019 the statement of faith was broadened to include all orthodox views of the return of Christ, including amillennial and postmillennial views, by replacing the word "premillennial" with the word "glorious." We believe in the glorious return of Jesus, we say.

If the amillennial view is new to you, as it will be to many in the EFCA, as you read my discussion of Article 9, I hope you'll see that I'm trying to take the Bible seriously and cooperate with the original intent of the authors—at least how I and many others understand it. To learn more about the amillennial view, I'd suggest watching the video "An Evening of Eschatology" produced by Desiring God and reading the books *The Bible and the Future* by Anthony Hoekema (Eerdmans, 1979, republished 1994) and *Kingdom Come: The Amillennial Alternative* by Sam Storms (Christian Focus, 2013).

The Process of Ordination

Ordination is the affirmation of God's call to pastoral ministry. It's also the verification of theological and moral fitness for ministry. Each denomination has its own process for ordination. Speaking in broad strokes, the process of ordination in the EFCA involves three steps:

> **Step 1:** Write a twenty-page paper that engages with the EFCA statement of faith and then defend your theology in a two-hour oral examination conducted by the credentialing council, which is composed of a dozen or so ordained local pastors.

> **Step 2:** Complete at least three years of healthy pastoral ministry in a local EFCA church.

> **Step 3:** Do "Step 1" again—except this round, everything is doubled: a forty-page paper and a four-hour exam.

On October 8, 2019, I completed the final step. And in case this isn't clear, I did pass.

The Backstory

Before launching into the paper, let me mention a few matters related to the publishing of this book.

First, with the exception of this preface and the changes in formatting, this book is largely my ordination paper as it was written, submitted, and approved. I updated a few things here and there and expanded the paper by 15% per feedback from others. But I didn't add near as much as I would have liked because I wanted this book to reflect the space requirements of ordination papers set by the EFCA. This is why a few of the sections at the end of the paper appear so sparse. With respect to formatting, I ditched the Times Roman 12-point double-spaced layout for the sake of readability. Also, you may wonder why I don't have any footnotes or quote theologians from the past and present. That's intentional. The requirements of the original paper do not allow for it.

Second, the discussion questions at the end of each section were not written by me. They were borrowed from the credentialing information provided on the EFCA website and were included with permission. The questions are intended to give those pursuing ordination a sense of the types of questions that should be answered in one's paper. I did my best to follow that advice.

Third, let me discuss the title. I titled this book *Once for all Delivered* as an allusion to the admonition Jude gives in the beginning of his epistle. "Beloved, although I was very eager to write to you about our common salvation," he writes, "I found it necessary to write appealing to you to contend for the faith that was once for all delivered to the saints" (1:3). Jude considered it necessary that Christians—not just professional clergy—contend for the faith. The word translated *contend* is only used here in the New Testament. One lexicon suggests that contend means "to exert intense effort on behalf of something" (Johannes P. Louw and Eugene A. Nida, *Greek-English Lexicon of the New Testament*). Christians are to exert intense effort to make sure that they understand the faith and others around them understand the faith as well. That's what the ordination process was for me—an attempt to clarify how I understand the faith once for all delivered.

But if that's what the title means, let me also share what the title does *not* mean. I'm well aware that my paper does not constitute the official position of the EFCA—let alone the official understanding of Christian theology—any more than any other approved ordination paper becomes our gold standard. I may be the first, but I don't assume first will mean best. I hoist my candle to join the floodlight.

Finally, while I prepared for my ordination exam, several people encouraged me to publish my paper, including those who sat on my council. I consented because I hoped that as others read my paper, perhaps I could offer them an opportunity to enjoy more of Jesus and the richness of his work on our behalf. And even at the points where others will judge that my words misstep and err, I hoped the book would stimulate deeper reflection. And if this happens, then *soli deo gloria*.

Benjamin Vrbicek
Harrisburg, Pennsylvania
December 2019

PART I

BIOGRAPHICAL SECTION

CONVERSION, CALL &

PREPARATION FOR

MINISTRY

I grew up in a Christian family but likely only embraced the externals of the faith until my junior year of college. Just prior to that time, everything started to unravel. My world—which revolved around academics, athletics, and a relationship with a girlfriend—fell apart. All three were letting me down. I was hurt, confused, and exhausted. In the spring of my junior year, by God's grace, I began attending a Bible study in the athletic department. After that semester I attended a Christian sports camp in Colorado. There I was surrounded by Christians who actually cared about all the things I knew I was supposed to care about but never did. They also seemed to have a deep joy, which I certainly did not. I left the camp with the determination to follow Christ; I ended my relationship with my longtime girlfriend and began reading the Bible. In those next few months, I saw my sin as not only hurtful to other people but offensive to God. I saw Jesus as the Savior whose death and resurrection was real and sufficient for my sins. Through repentance and faith, eternal life was offered, which I gladly received.

Over the next few years, God nudged me slowly but assuredly into the ministry; I led a Bible study on campus and spoke at youth gatherings. Fifteen years ago, an EFCA pastor helped me to preach my first sermon. I have sensed my call to ministry through my own passion and gifting in ministry, which others around me have confirmed. It has been a blessing to use and refine these gifts during my time at Covenant Theological Seminary in St. Louis, MO (2006–2011, MDiv) and volunteer pastoral ministry at Salem EFCA in St. Louis, MO (2008–2011), New Life Bible Fellowship in Tucson, AZ (2011–2014), and Community EFCA in Harrisburg, PA (2014–present). At Community I serve as the lead pastor of a church of around 300 adults.

Over the last few years, a growing extension of my local church pastoral ministry has been my writing ministry. I blog regularly on my own site and occasionally have articles published elsewhere (e.g., The Gospel Coalition, Desiring God, For the Church, and EFCA NOW). I've also authored or coauthored three self-published books and one book with a small Christian publisher:

More People to Love: How the Bible Starts in a Garden and Ends in a City and What That Means for You

Don't Just Send a Resume: How to Find the Right Job in a Local Church

Struggle Against Porn: 29 Diagnostic Questions for Your Head and Heart

Enduring Grace: 21 Days with The Apostle Peter

Blogging for God's Glory in a Clickbait World: A Christian's Guide (forthcoming fall 2020)

My wife, Brooke, and I married in 2005. We have six children, currently ages two to thirteen. Brooke grew up in a Christian home and became a Christian at a young age. She has been supportive of my call into full-time ministry and serves regularly in the local church. She does not work outside the home but most certainly works awfully hard within our home!

PART II

DOCTRINAL
SECTION

GOD

1. We believe in one God, Creator of all things, holy, infinitely perfect, and eternally existing in a loving unity of three equally divine Persons: the Father, the Son and the Holy Spirit. Having limitless knowledge and sovereign power, God has graciously purposed from eternity to redeem a people for Himself and to make all things new for His own glory.

I am not sure I could restate a succinct trinitarian affirmation better than the way it's communicated in our statement of faith: "eternally existing in a loving unity of three equally divine Persons: the Father, the Son and the Holy Spirit." Each word has consequence and clarifies what Christians mean by Trinity. God's existence never begins nor ends (Ps 102:24–27; Dan 4:34–35; Acts 17:24–25). Love is shared among the members of the Godhead (Jn 17:24), a love that flows to believers through our faith in Christ and then becomes the pattern for how we interact with others, especially other believers (Jn 13:34; Eph 5:1–2). An economic submission exists among the Trinity where, for example, the Son submits to the Father's will in the plan of salvation (see esp. the gospel of John). However, the three members of the Trinity are equal in essence; no ontological submission exists within the Trinity (Gen 1:26; Mt 28:19–20; Jn 1:1–18). They are persons, *not*

7

forces or things (2 Cor 13:14; cf. Acts 5:3–4). They are Father (Dt 32:6; Rm 8:15), Son (Jn 1:14; Heb 1:2, 5), and Holy Spirit (Jn 16:7–15; Rm 8:9). This is the Trinitarian God represented in Scripture, as well as the historic, orthodox view of the church in our creeds, particularly the Athanasian Creed. Ancient and modern heresies regarding the Trinity tend to arise from the denial of one or more of these truths. For example, modalism teaches that God expresses himself in three different modes that are not eternally distinct and coexistent. The Father couldn't be singing his praise of his Son while the Son was being baptized and the Spirit was resting upon the Son if they are not distinct persons (Lk 3:21–22).

The biblical story begins describing God as Creator (Gen 1:1ff). In the Genesis creation account, as well as other places (Jn 1:3; Rm 9:20ff; Col 1:16–17; Ps 19:1–6), we learn many important truths about God as Creator, such as God created for his glory, creation is good—indeed, very good—and God remains distinct from his creation, having authority over all he has made. Perhaps God created the earth in a sequence of literal 24-hour days with the appearance of age, but I do not think this is a necessary view within a historical, grammatical, redemptive approach to reading Scripture, which is my hermeneutic. I favor an old earth interpretation, understood in the *analogical day* view, which teaches that God used the analogy of days to communicate to us without specifying duration. In this view, the days are something of an anthropomorphism, that is, our human week becomes a pattern of the divine week of creation. Also worth noting is the non-literal use of *day* in Genesis 2:4 and 2:17. I do not, however, believe in theistic evolution. A million monkeys clacking away on a million typewriters for a million years will never compose *MacBeth*, and if they did, by definition, it wouldn't have been done *ex nihilo.* The earth may be old, but humanity is young and began with a historical Adam and Eve. When biblical authors speak of Adam and Eve, they speak of them as people who actually lived (1 Chr 1:1; Matt 19:4–6; Lk 3:38; Rm 5:12–17; 2 Cor 11:3; 1 Tim 2:13–14; Jude 1:14). A historical Adam proves central to the gospel because, without a historical Adam who represents all of humanity as our federal head, we could not also have a second Adam, the Christ, who represents us as humans (Rm 5:12–21).

A seminal passage on God's nature and attributes is Exodus 34:6–7, as seen in the way its wording reverberates through so many other, later passages (to name just a few passages, Num 14:18; 2 Chr 30:9; Neh 9:17; Ps 86:15; 103:8; Jer 32:18; Joel 2:13; Micah 7:18; and Nahum 1:3). In the Exodus passage, we see that having a vibrant understanding of God's attributes is important for two reasons. First, only through our understanding of God's attributes can we specify which God, among all the supposed gods, we have in view. We believe in "the LORD, the LORD, a God merciful and gracious, slow to anger . . ."—*not* the golden calf, *not* Pharaoh, *not* nature, *not* other national deities. Second, proper understanding of God leads to proper worship of him. When God hid Moses between two rocks so Moses would only glimpse God's backside—not even his face—Moses quickly bowed his forehead to the dirt and worshiped (Ex 33:23; 34:8).

A few of God's other attributes include his oneness (Dt 6:4; Mk 12:29), holiness (Is 6:3; 1 Pet 1:15), limitless knowledge (Ps 139:1–16; Is 46:10; Jn 21:17), and sovereign power (Jer 32:17; Eph 1:11). In the traditional discussion of communicable and incommunicable attributes, we can sometimes overstate the degree to which God shares or does not share an attribute, but I affirm that aseity (Acts 17:24–25), immutability and eternality (Ps 102:25–27), omniscience (Ps 139:1–6), and omnipresence (Ps 139:7–12) are far less shared with humans, while attributes such as God's love (1 Jn 4:7), justice (1 Pet 1:17), and wisdom (Prov 6:6) are more recognizably shared.

With respect to God's limitless knowledge, some argue against this from the handful of passages that seem to suggest God does not know the future (Jer 19:5) and that he occasionally must repent, famously in passages such as Genesis 6:6–7 and 1 Samuel 15:11. Worth noting is that the very same 1 Samuel 15 passage also says God will not repent (v. 29; cf. Num 23:19). Better approaches to the apparent contradiction exist than the solutions offered by open theism, which teaches the future is open, meaning God created a world of real possibilities where our actions determine the future. It is far better to see God's appearance of change as the revealing of his new posture toward a person or situation, not as "change" required because God is morally deficient or caught unaware. Our actions only change God in so much as he has sovereignly ordained them to change him. That is to say that when God ordains something, he also ordains the means. An abundance of verses teach that God knows not only the actual future exhaustively (Is 42:9; Jn 13:19) but that he even knows hypothetical futures, as when Jesus states that he knows what people in Tyre, Sidon, and Sodom would have done (re: repent) had they been alive during his early ministry (Mt 11:20–25).

A chief element of what makes God's glory so glorious is his purpose, as this article states, to "redeem a people for Himself," meaning he graciously purchases sinners from the due punishment of sin through the costly death of the Son (Titus 2:14; 1 Pet 1:18–19). Not only has God purposed to redeem sinners but he will renew creation as well. The Bible speaks of creation as groaning until its day of redemption (Rm 8:18–25). Some disagreement occurs among Christians as to the sense in which the new heavens and earth will be "new." I do not take new to mean that God will scrap all of his creation and start over, even though a verse like 2 Peter 3:10 could be so understood. Instead, I take new in the sense of *r*enewed and fitted appropriately for the city that has no death, mourning, crying, or pain (Rev 21:4). Because creation will be renewed, we should treat the earth and its resources with care, as Adam and Eve were first called to do (Gen 1:28; 2:15). If God values something, so should we.

Discussion Questions

Creator and Creation

1. What does it mean that God is the Creator? Why is this important?

2. How do you interpret Genesis 1?

3. How does your interpretation of Genesis 1 relate to your view of Scripture?

Attributes

4. Describe the essential attributes of God. Why is it necessary, or important, to have a working understanding of the nature and attributes of God?

5. What does it mean that God is holy? What are the implications of his holiness?

Trinity

6. Describe the doctrine of the Trinity. How do you teach this doctrine from Scripture?

7. What is the importance of the truth that God, as "three equally divine Persons," eternally exists "in a loving unity"?

8. Describe one contemporary denial of the doctrine of the Trinity. Why is it heretical?

Limitless Knowledge and Sovereign Power (Open Theism)

9. What does it mean that God has "limitless knowledge and sovereign power"? Why is this significant in contemporary debates about God?

Gracious Purpose to Redeem

10. What is the significance of God graciously purposing from eternity to redeem a people for himself?

Make All Things New for His Glory

11. How does redemption relate to the creation? What impact does your view have for our present stewardship of the earth's resources?

THE BIBLE

2. We believe that God has spoken in the Scriptures, both Old and New Testaments, through the words of human authors. As the verbally inspired Word of God, the Bible is without error in the original writings, the complete revelation of His will for salvation, and the ultimate authority by which every realm of human knowledge and endeavor should be judged. Therefore, it is to be believed in all that it teaches, obeyed in all that it requires, and trusted in all that it promises.

Knowledge of God comes to humans in two primary ways: in general revelation to all humans through God's creation, including a person's conscience (Ps 19:1-6; Rm 2:14-15), and in special revelation through the Bible and the person of Christ, the Word made flesh (Jn 1:14). Although people misinterpret and even suppress general revelation (Rm 1:18ff; 1 Tim 4:2), from general revelation we learn of God's creative power and gain a sense of right and wrong. General revelation, however, does not communicate the explicit content of the gospel, whereas special revelation does. The Bible is sufficient to reveal who God is and how we must relate to him; clear enough to be understood; authoritative on all matters to which it speaks; and necessary for people to know God, his gospel, and how to live a life pleasing to him.

The relationship between God's authorship and human authorship is best understood in this way: God inspired human authors to communicate in a way consistent with their humanness (e.g., education and linguistic ability, temperament and passion, life and work experience) but also in a way that elevates the human author's words far beyond natural ability (Dt 18:18; Lk 1:1-4; Heb 1:1-2). I see this view of biblical inspiration displayed, for example, when Jesus interchangeably refers to Old Testament passages in Mark 7:9-13 with the phrases "the commandment of God," "for Moses said," and "the word of God" (cf. Ex 20:12; 21:17). In other words, what Moses said can also be described as what God said. The Bible also takes direct quotes from the mouth of God and says Scripture speaks, as when Paul writes, "the Scripture ... preached the gospel beforehand to Abraham, saying, 'In you shall all the nations be blessed'" (Gal 3:8; cf. Gn 12:3).

Additionally, it is not merely the overarching biblical story and related concepts that are inspired but that the individual words themselves are purposely selected by human authors under the superintendence of God. We call this verbal plenary inspiration (Mt 5:18; 2 Pet 1:20-21). Therefore, we speak no falsehood when we affirm the Bible as infallible and inerrant in the original manuscripts, because God himself is absolutely truthful and without error (Mt 5:18; Titus 1:1-2). Infallible means the words of God's inspired prophets and apostles, when giving revelation under the inspiration of the Spirit, cannot fail (Is 55:1). Inerrant means the Bible—like God—is truthful and without error concerning all matters to which it speaks.

The canon composed of the 66 books of the Old and New Testaments (hereafter, OT and NT) is complete, meaning we should never add to the canon. It might seem odd to ask the question "How does the Bible speak about itself with respect to its own completeness?" because the Bible has many different human authors. How then can it be said to speak singularly? But asking and answering this question bears fruit. The Bible speaks about its completeness and canonicity in several ways.

First, the Bible repeatedly intimates its own inscripturation (Dt 31:24–26; Jos 24:26; 2 Chr 34:14; Jer 30:2; Rev 22:18–19).

Second, the meaning of the "last days" implies a closed canon. Biblically speaking, the last days are the entire period of time between the outpouring of the Holy Spirit at Pentecost and Jesus's second coming (Acts 2:17; Joel 2; Jam 5:3). The way Hebrews 1:1–2 uses the phrase *last days* (cf. Acts 2:17 and Jam 5:3) and Jude 1:3 speaks of "the faith once for all delivered" indicates a definitive and concluding speaking of God through Jesus and, by extension, the first-century apostles authorized by Jesus as his messengers (1 Cor 2:13; Eph 2:19–20; 2 Pet 1:21; 3:2).

Third, the intertestamental books often called the Apocrypha were not considered canonical to Jesus and the early church (or to the Jews who wrote them), but the OT and NT most certainly were. For example, 1 Maccabees, which is not canonical, acknowledges that people have no word from an authorized messenger of God, a touchstone of canonicity (1 Mac 4:45–45; 9:27; 14:41; cf. Am 8:11). It seems Jesus acknowledges the lack of authority of the Apocrypha by snubbing the intertestamental martyrs when he mentions OT martyrs in Luke 11:45–52 but makes no mention of the martyrs listed in the Apocrypha. On top of this, the NT authors seamlessly use the Greek word *graphē* (Scripture) to place OT quotations alongside the NT in 1 Timothy 5:18 and 2 Peter 3:16, showing the writings of both the OT and NT were considered *graphē*, that is, canonical Scripture.

Fourth, there is an internal coherence among the books in the canon. The individual parts see themselves as just that—individual parts of the one, greater story.

Finally, the early church fathers recognized the Bible as having a self-authenticating purity and power not evident in later writings (e.g., early church councils, the correspondence of church fathers, and the continued written testimony of Christians). A letter from Athanasius in AD 367 contained a list of all 27 books we affirm as the NT canon, which is also the same list affirmed at the Council of Carthage in 397.

To approach canonicity using the common shorthand, the fourfold test for canonicity is apostolic origin, universal acceptance, liturgical use, and consistent message. It's unlikely that the church will discover an ancient letter proved to be written by an apostle, say one of Paul's additional letters to the church in Corinth alluded to in 1 Corinthians 5:9 and 16:3. But even if a newly discovered letter passed the tests of apostolic origin and consistent message, a long-hidden letter could hardly be said to have received universal acceptance.

While we do not have the autographs, the abundance of extant copies of the original manuscripts assures us of the reliability of modern Bible translations, which come from an eclectic mix of the best manuscripts. And where slight discrepancies do exist, no major doctrine stands or falls on the variations. For all these reasons, I do not think we mislead people when at our church, upon reading the sermon text, a pastor says, "This is God's Word; thanks be to God."

Before leaving the topic of inspiration and canonicity, it might be helpful to comment on the longer ending of Mark and the passage in John about the woman caught in adultery. It seems best to conclude neither passage was original, though both passages when rightly interpreted in light of the rest of the Bible do not contradict any doctrine. A careful reading of Mark 16:18 sees not the command to pick up snakes and drink poison but a promise of protection, something Paul experienced in Acts 28. And the story in John's gospel is consistent with the actions of Jesus in the rest of the Gospels and was likely a real event, just one not originally included by John (cf. Jn 21:25). Modern Bible translations rightly inform readers that the earliest manuscripts did not include either passage.

"Red-letter Christians," who purport to take the commands of Jesus seriously, commit a modern canonical error worth discussing. Their emphasis on loving our neighbors *and* our enemies as well as serving fellow believers *and* the least of these are themes less often preached and practiced in affluent, majority-culture Christianity. But to pit the direct quotes of Jesus—the so-called red-letter parts of the Bible—against the rest of the Bible is foolish. Jesus trained and commissioned his apostles to be his authorized spokesmen empowered by the Holy Spirit (Jn 16:12–15; Acts 1:8); therefore, the content that Peter wrote in his letters or that John wrote in his gospel, even the non-red parts, is no less authoritative than, say, the sermon on the mount. The error of red-letter Christianity is not unlike breaking light bulbs on a Christmas tree: if you take away lights, the whole strand stops working properly. The complete 66 books of the Bible work in concert, not in isolation or opposition to each other. To take Jesus at his word means to take his authorized spokesmen at their words because he commissioned them; and not only that, but listening to Jesus well means acknowledging that the OT testifies to him (Jn 5:39).

In light of everything written above, it is right to speak of the Bible as the "ultimate authority," meaning nothing stands over the Bible to judge, interpret, or critique it (Jn 17:17; 2 Tim 3:16–17). Scripture is sufficient to provide everything we need for life and godliness (2 Pet 1:3). This should not be misunderstood to say every part of the Bible is equally clear to all people, but it is to affirm that everything required for an ordinary Christian to be faithful to God can be clearly understood in the Bible. Therefore we must be those who "[believe] all that it teaches, [obey] all that it requires, and [trust] all that it promises," and invite others to do the same. Holding fast to this view of Scripture leads to the blessing of God's people and the advancement of his kingdom, as well as energizing my own labors in preaching and teaching.

Discussion Questions

Old and New Testaments, Canon

1. Explain your understanding of the development of the canon of Scripture.

2. What are the canonical issues involved with Mark 16:9–20? John 7:53–8:11?

3. Describe one modern day canonical dispute. How would you respond to it?

Inspiration

4. How do you understand the process of inspiration and its result? What implications does this doctrine have on your life and ministry?

5. What do the words "verbally inspired" mean?

Inerrancy

6. What is "inerrancy," and why is it important? What does it mean that this concept is applied to "the original writings"? How do inerrancy and infallibility relate?

7. Are modern translations of the Bible inerrant? How are they reliable?

Complete Revelation

8. What is the difference between general and special revelation?

9. How helpful is general revelation when it comes to knowing God, viz. is it salvific?

10. What does the clarity of Scripture mean and what are its implications?

11. What does it mean, both doctrinally and practically, that the Scriptures are sufficient?

Ultimate Authority

12. In relation to how and what we know, why is it important to state that the Scripture, God's Word, is "the ultimate authority by which every realm of human knowledge and endeavor should be judged"?

Believed, Obeyed, Trusted

13. Regarding the truth of God's Word, what is to be your response? What is the implication for your life and ministry?

THE HUMAN CONDITION

3. We believe that God created Adam and Eve in His image, but they sinned when tempted by Satan. In union with Adam, human beings are sinners by nature and by choice, alienated from God, and under His wrath. Only through God's saving work in Jesus Christ can we be rescued, reconciled and renewed.

G enesis 1:26–27 states that God created Adam and Eve in his image and likeness (cf. Gen 5:1; 9:6; Jam 3:9). Throughout the centuries theologians have attempted to clarify precisely what attribute, or perhaps several attributes, humans are bestowed with that most corresponds to the image of our Creator, thus making us distinct from animals. However, it is difficult and perhaps unwise to be too specific about what the *imago dei* means. But from the way *image* is used in passages like Exodus 20:4, 1 Samuel 6:5, 11, and Ezekiel 23:14 and *likeness* is used in 2 Kings 16:10, 2 Chronicles 4:3, 4, Psalm 58:4, and Mark 12:16–17, I conclude there are many ways we are *like* God and many ways we *represent* him. Some examples of this include the way humans have moral, spiritual, mental, artistic, intelligent, and relational capacities. Resisting the impulse to define the image of God singularly on any one trait protects us from the error of too narrowly limiting what it means to be human. So, for example, if we intricately link the image of God with human intelligence, we could get to the place where a person with severely diminished mental capacities ceases being human, or at a minimum becomes in some way sub-human, which of course is wrong.

Additionally, to be human is to be in union with the first human, Adam—a historical person, created by God as our representative at the headwaters of humanity. However, when tempted by Satan, Adam and Eve disobeyed God. As our federal head, Adam's sin plunged himself and all subsequent generations into a state of rebellion against God (Gen 2–3; Rm 5:12–21; 1 Cor 15:21–22). Our rebellious state is both inherited and also a result of individual choices (Ps 51:5; Is 6:5; Rm 5:12; Eph 2:1–2). We are not sinners simply because we sin; rather, we sin because we are sinners. Our inherited sin nature means people are born alienated from God and under his wrath (Rm 1:18; 2:5; 3:9–19; 3:23; 5:10; Eph 2:3). The wrath of God is his intense hatred of sin and just punishment of sin (Rm 1:18ff; Rev 19:15). While our rebellious bent severely tarnishes the image of God in us, the fall does not entirely eradicate the image of God but remains in believers and unbelievers alike (Gen 5:1; 9:6; Ps 8; Jam 3:9). This means every person—no matter how depraved or having physical and mental challenges—has dignity, value, and worth. The doctrine of the *imago dei* has many implications, but to name just a few of them we could say that Christians should advocate for life from its first beginning to its natural end and for the just treatment of all, including immigrants, refugees, criminals, and prisoners of war.

In the Bible, Satan is described in various ways: sometimes as a whispering serpent and other times as a roaring lion, sometimes as a thief and other times as a masquerading angel of light. But whether stalking or slinking, he is a deceptive and dangerous enemy (Gen 3; 1 Pet 5:8; Jn 10:10; 2 Cor 11:14). Everything God created in Genesis 1 was good, but somewhere before Satan's mysterious entrance into the biblical story in Genesis 3, there must have been an angelic rebellion of sorts, presumably led by Satan. Indeed, an evil angelic rebellion seems alluded to in passages like 2 Peter 2:4 and Jude 1:6. (It's possible but not my conviction that Satan and his fall are also alluded to in the exalted descriptions of the King of Babylon in Isaiah 14:12–15 and the King of Tyre in Ezekiel 26–28.) Whatever his origins, the Bible describes Satan's activity in many places, including Genesis 3, Job 1–2, and the wilderness temptations of Christ in the Gospels (Mt 4; Mk 1; Lk 4). Satan's evil reign often casts a dark shadow over human sin and suffering even when he is not named explicitly (cf. 1 Jn 5:19). We see this mysterious interplay in passages like Ephesians 2, where Paul describes Satan as "the spirit that is now at work in the sons of disobedience" and passages like Luke 22:31, where Jesus alludes to a behind-the-scenes demand of Satan that we would have known nothing about if we had not been explicitly told about the demand. Affirming that Satan has a role in human sin does not excuse our culpability, but it does enlarge our understanding of why the world is so broken, even stirring our empathy for those ensnared and captured by the devil (2 Tim 2:26). One day, his reign will end (Rev 20:9–10). Indeed, Satan's inferiority to God is such that upon the return of Christ, Jesus will kill Satan's lawless one simply with the breath of his mouth (2 Thes 2:8–9; cf. Is 11:4). With the ease you and I blow dust from our laptops, Jesus will defeat the deceiver of the whole world and the accuser of the brethren. Though "The

Prince of Darkness grim, we tremble not for him; his rage we can endure, for lo, his doom is sure."

The great hope of the gospel is that through God's saving work in Jesus Christ we can be rescued, reconciled, and renewed. These three sweeping terms highlight themes of the redemptive story: rescued means sin and Satan once held us captive (Jn 8:34; Rm 6:20; Col 2:15; 2 Tim 2:26); reconciled means God mends our relationship with him (2 Cor 5:18-21); and renewed means that, although we were dead in our sins and totally depraved—that is, sin tarnishes even our best deeds and prevents us from doing spiritual good before a holy God (Rm 6:23; 14:23; Eph 2:1)—God restores us, both progressively in this life and completely in the next (Rm 8:18ff; 2 Cor 5:17; Phil 3:21; 1 Jn 3:2).

Discussion Questions

Adam and Eve, Image of God

1. What does it mean that Adam and Eve were created in the image of God? What are the implications of this doctrine for us today?

Fall

2. How do you understand the fall of humanity and its effects?

3. What does the fall teach us about the nature of sin?

Satan

4. Who is Satan, and what role does he play in the fall of Adam and Eve? What is he working to accomplish today?

Union with Adam, Sinners by Nature and by Choice

5. How do you understand "union with Adam"? What does it mean that we "are sinners by nature and by choice"? Briefly explain these concepts from Romans 5:12–21.

Alienation from God

6. What does it mean that we are alienated from God?

God's Wrath

7. What does the wrath of God mean and what is its significance?

Rescued, Reconciled and Renewed

8. From what are we rescued? To whom are we reconciled? How are we renewed?

9. Why is it important to state exclusively that this work is accomplished only through God's saving work in Jesus Christ?

JESUS CHRIST

4. We believe that Jesus Christ is God incarnate, fully God and fully man, one Person in two natures. Jesus—Israel's promised Messiah—was conceived through the Holy Spirit and born of the virgin Mary. He lived a sinless life, was crucified under Pontius Pilate, arose bodily from the dead, ascended into heaven and sits at the right hand of God the Father as our High Priest and Advocate.

As with the doctrine of the Trinity, Christians can struggle to understand Jesus's full divinity and humanity, yet faithful exposition of the Bible leads decidedly toward the hypostatic union. In his incarnation, the second person of the Trinity, the Son of God, became flesh: he was born, increased in wisdom and stature (Lk 2:52), ate (Mt 9:10-11), slept (Mk 4:38), got tired (Jn 4:6), felt sadness and wept (Jn 11:35), and experienced great pain and died (Mk 15:37). But Jesus also remained fully God: he was sinless; fulfilled the law in every positive way (Mt 5:17); "before Abraham" (Jn 8:58); performed miracles, including raising the dead; was understood by the religious leaders to make claims of divinity (Jn 10:31–33); didn't rebuke Thomas when he called Jesus his Lord and his God (Jn 20:28); made "I am" statements of himself knowing full well their OT connection to the name of

God (Jn 6:35; 10:7; 10:11; 11:25; 14:6; 15:5; 18:6; cf. Ex 3:14); and in addition to all this, applied the lofty claims of Daniel 7:13–14 and Psalm 110:1 to himself (Mt 26:64). Christ's dual nature allowed him to be our Savior: in his humanity he identifies with us, and in his divinity he is a worthy sacrifice in a way no human could be. A number of heresies regarding the nature of Christ arose in the early church that denied in some way Christ's two natures in one person. Some such heresies were Nestorianism (two natures but not a unified person), Eutychianism (not the union of two natures but the blending of two), Apollinarianism (like a man but not quite a man), and Docetism (seeming to be a man but not). Scripture precludes these views of Christ and various church councils rejected them as unbiblical.

Some have taken the RSV's rendering of "emptied himself" in Philippians 2:6–7 to mean that Jesus somehow became less than God in the incarnation. However, the emptying did not entail the relinquishing of Christ's divinity but rather the temporary setting aside of his glory to take on the form of a servant. The glory Jesus set aside, by the way, has now been returned to him by the Father (Jn 17:5); there is nothing, including the timing of his return, that the risen and ascended Christ does not know as he sits on the throne of the universe.

The incarnation began with the virgin conception (Is 7:14; Mt 1:20) and proved critical in God's uniting the humanity and deity of Jesus. Yes, Jesus was conceived, something common to humans, but his conception was a supernatural conception, a beautiful and divine interruption into the only pattern humanity has ever known: sinners begetting other sinners. In a mysterious way, the virgin birth kept Jesus from inheriting the sin nature inherited by every other human since Adam (Gen 3;

28

Rm 5:12–21; 1 Cor 15:21–22). Our salvation required a sinless Savior because only a pure, spotless Lamb could die in our place as a worthy sacrifice (Jn 1:29; 1 Pet 3:18). A sinner dying for other sinners saves no one.

To address Christ's sinlessness from another vantage point, we can speak of Christ's perfect obedience, which theologians sometimes view in two complementary parts, these being his active and passive obedience. We call Christ's obedience to every aspect of the law and will of God his active obedience. The passive obedience of Christ refers to every aspect of his sin-bearing obedience, which of course culminates in the cross but was also experienced as Christ, though the perfect God-man, experienced all that comes with living in a broken world. In his earthly ministry, Jesus experienced temptations, which were doubtless many and varied (cf. the wilderness temptations in Mt 4:1–11 or the way Satan spoke through Peter to tempt Jesus to forgo the mission of the cross in Mt 16:23). The book of Hebrews even speaks of Jesus being tempted "in every respect," which doesn't mean he experienced every single possible temptation but that he did experience enough of the cross-section of life that he can identify and even sympathize with us (4:15). In his humanity, these temptations were real despite that he has no sin nature. Thankfully, in his divinity, Jesus was not able to sin, which we call his impeccability.

Calling Jesus the promised Messiah of Israel means the person and work of Jesus is part of, and indeed the continuation of, a story long ago begun (Gen 3:16; 2 Sam 7:11ff; Mt 1:1ff; Gal 4:4). Many in Jesus's day expected the Messiah, but most did not expect a Messiah who would be humiliated before his exultation, yet this was God's foreordained plan. Prior to the crucifixion, Jesus predicted his death often in both subtle ways (e.g., the parable of tenants killing the landowner's son in Mt 21:33–46) and overt ways (cf. the passion predictions in Mk 8:3; 9:30–32; 10:32–34). But Jesus also taught that he had authority to lay his life down and the power to take it up again (Jn 10:17–18). When this power was exercised in a bodily resurrection (not a merely spiritual or metaphorical resurrection), Jesus demonstrated that he was the Promised One who would lead his people and usher in the time in which light would shine to the nations beginning the great ingathering of Gentiles (Is 49:12; 60:3; Lk 2:32; Acts 26:23; Rm 15:8–9). In our present era Jesus sits at the right hand of God as the exalted Davidic heir (2 Sam 7:14ff; 2 Tim 2:8) until his enemies are made a footstool (Ps 110:1; Mt 26:64; Acts 2:35; Eph 1:20) while he exercises the authority given to him (Mt 28:18) to advance his kingdom until his pending return (Mt 24:30–31). The session of Christ as our king (Acts 1:9; Rev 20:1–6) and his ongoing ministry as our Great High Priest (Heb 8; 10:19–22) and Advocate (1 Jn 2:1–2) give me hope as I labor to be conformed to the image of Christ amidst the brokenness of our world.

Discussion Questions

God Incarnate, Fully God and Fully Man, One Person in Two Natures

1. What is the significance of the incarnation? Why was it necessary for our salvation?

2. Explain your understanding of the Hypostatic Union of Jesus Christ. How do you understand Phil 2:7?

3. What were some of the Christological heresies as the early church attempted to understand and explain the hypostatic union?

Israel's Promised Messiah (Relation to Prophecy)

4. Why is it important that Jesus be known as "Israel's promised Messiah"? What is its importance for our understanding of Jesus? What about our understanding of the Bible?

Virgin Birth

5. What is the virgin birth, why is it essential, and what is its significance for our understanding of christology and soteriology?

Sinless Life, Crucifixion

6. What is the significance of Jesus's perfect obedience (both active and passive) for our salvation?

7. Could Jesus have sinned? How do you understand the temptations?

8. Why did Jesus die?

Bodily Resurrection, Ascension and Session

9. What is the importance of Jesus's resurrection?

10. How do you understand the nature of Jesus's resurrection body?

11. What is the significance of the ascension and session of Jesus Christ?

High Priest and Advocate

12. What is the significance of Jesus's ministry as High Priest and Advocate and how does this affect your life and ministry?

THE WORK OF CHRIST

5. We believe that Jesus Christ, as our representative and substitute, shed His blood on the cross as the perfect, all-sufficient sacrifice for our sins. His atoning death and victorious resurrection constitute the only ground for salvation.

J esus died as our representative and substitute, which means his death was a penal substitutionary atonement: Jesus took upon himself the punishment our sins deserved (Is 53:5–6; Mk 10:45; Gal 3:13; 1 Pet 2:24). His death was sufficient for all but effectually only for his elect (Mt 1:21; Jn 10:15; 15:13; Acts 20:28). What an undeserved joy we have as Christians knowing that in dying for his bride, Jesus did something special for us that he does not do for all (cf. Eph 5:25). Moreover, Jesus does not simply atone for our sins but also purchases the power that makes our salvation not merely a possibility people *can* experience but the reality believers *will* experience (Acts 20:28; Rm 8:31–34; Gal 1:4; Eph 1:11–14; Titus 2:14); his atonement is limited in scope but not in power. Related to the power of Christ's atonement is God's irresistible grace. To affirm God's grace as irresistible does not mean God's grace can't be resisted. The Pharisees did precisely this in Luke 7:30. We do the same each time we sin. But what I cherish in irresistible grace is God's ability, when he so chooses, to subdue all of our resistance to his love and deadness to true joy.

Since we're talking about salvation, I should clarify what I mean. Salvation has broad meaning in the Bible, such as salvation from enemies in war or salvation from a life-threatening illness. But with respect to the atonement, salvation carries the idea of being delivered from God's wrath (1 Thes 1:10) by God crushing his own Son in our place (Is 53:10) to bring his people near and reconcile them to himself (Eph 2:13; 1 Pet 3:18; 2 Cor 5:19). Our salvation is from God, by God, to God. God gives us eternal, abundant life with him when we only deserved eternal death and separation from him.

When discussing salvation from God's wrath, it is helpful to define both expiation and propitiation which differentiate along these lines: expiation is an action that cleanses from sin and takes away guilt, while propitiation focuses on the appeasement of God's wrath. Several key passages inform the discussion of expiation and propitiation (e.g., Lev 17:11 and other OT sacrificial passages; Rm 3:25; Heb 9:5; 1 Jn 2:2; 4:10). While both concepts are biblical, it is worth pointing out that a sinner's guilt cannot be removed without the appeasement of God's wrath and the shedding of blood by taking a life (cf. Lev 17:11 and Heb 9:22). Because penal substitutionary atonement and the discussion of the appeasement of wrath can provoke wrong views of God, as though he were cold and calculating, I should mention that the act of atonement itself does not make God love us; God has loved his people from before the creation of the world (Eph 1:4–5). Atonement graciously flows out of his love, not the other way around.

The exclusivity and necessity of Jesus's death need to be asserted not only because the Bible teaches this but also because of increasing cultural pressure to regulate religious claims to mere situational truthfulness—*if that's true for you, great; but it's not true for me.* Only one way leads to God in reconciliation, namely, faith in the finished work of Jesus's atoning death and victorious resurrection (Acts 4:12; 2 Thes 1:8). His resurrection is victorious because in rising from the dead, Christ achieved victory over sin, death, and evil (1 Cor 15:54–57; Col 2:15). Christ's resurrection affirms his claims (e.g., Jn 3:18–22; 10:19), attests to the Father's approval (Acts 13:30; Heb 1:8–9), and assures our own resurrection (Rm 4:5–6).

Discussion Questions

Representative and Substitute

1. What is it about Jesus's person and work that accomplishes our salvation?

2. What does it mean that Jesus is "our representative and substitute"?

Shed Blood on the Cross

3. Why was Jesus's shed blood necessary for our salvation?

4. Why is the centrality of the cross essential?

Once for all Delivered

Perfect, All-Sufficient Sacrifice for Sin

5. What is the significance of Christ's sacrificial death being "perfect" and "all-sufficient"? What is the value and necessity of his death?

6. How does the fact that this is the only way in which our sin is addressed compare with those embracing a wider hope of salvation beyond Christ and his work?

Atonement, Propitiation, Expiation, Redemption, Reconciliation

7. What is atonement? Define propitiation and expiation, and explain the difference.

8. Define redemption (cf. article 1). What does it mean to be reconciled to God, and what is its significance?

9. What is your understanding of 2 Corinthians 5:21? Explain your view of "imputation."

Victorious Resurrection

10. Why is Jesus's resurrection considered as an element of our salvation?

11. What is the significance that Jesus's resurrection is "victorious"? Who and what did Jesus overcome?

Only Ground of Salvation

12. What does it mean that Jesus's work is the "only ground for salvation"?

13. What does "salvation" mean biblically? Explain your understanding of it.

THE HOLY SPIRIT

6. We believe that the Holy Spirit, in all that He does, glorifies the Lord Jesus Christ. He convicts the world of its guilt. He regenerates sinners, and in Him they are baptized into union with Christ and adopted as heirs in the family of God. He also indwells, illuminates, guides, equips and empowers believers for Christ-like living and service.

Though previously stated in my discussion of Article 1, it bears repeating that the Holy Spirit is the divine, third person of the Trinity, not a force or thing (Acts 5:3–4; cf. the way Paul interchanges "God's temple" and "God's Spirit" in 1 Cor 3:16 and then "temple of the Holy Spirit" in 6:19). The Holy Spirit is alluded to, of course, in all the places the Trinity is alluded to in the OT (e.g., "us" in Gen 1:26; 11:7), but the OT explicitly mentions many variations of the phrase "Spirit of God." For example, in the second verse of the Bible we read of the Spirit "hovering over the face of the waters." Additionally, the specific phrasing of the "Holy Spirit" is mentioned rather famously in Psalm 51:11, while the NT mentions the title more frequently. The Spirit is also called by the epithet *Paraklēton*, variously translated as helper, advocate, counselor, and comforter (Jn 14:16; also said of Christ in 1 Jn 2:1).

In the OT the Spirit of God seems to function intermittently in the lives of various people, most of whom were believers. Cases like Saul make me hesitant to say *only* in believers. I've preached slowly and expositionally through 1 and 2 Samuel, and I'm not so sure even Saul's good start, upon close examination, is actually all that good. His decline, I suspect, reveals the true Saul. Regardless, in the OT the Holy Spirit functions intermittently when he comes upon a leader during a crisis (e.g., Jdg 6:34), a craftsman building (Ex 31:3), or a prophet prophesying (e.g., Is 61:1; Ez 8:3; 11:24). Perhaps God's Spirit worked in and among OT believers in a more abiding way, but we don't have many indications from the Scriptures that this was the case, though possibly a passage such as Isaiah 63:10–11 hints at this. Consider, as well, a passage such as Deuteronomy 10:16 where OT saints are told to circumcise the foreskins of their hearts or Deuteronomy 30:6 where Moses tells people about to cross the dry Jordan River that the Lord will circumcise their hearts (cf. Jer 4:4; Ez 44:7–9). Is not "circumcision of the heart" akin to regeneration language? If so, this makes one wonder to what extent the average OT believer had the Spirit. Speaking of OT Jews, Paul certainly links the work of the Spirit and circumcision in Romans 2:28–29. All this to say, I'm unsatisfied with the common statement "Today, we have the Spirit and back then they did not." It's more complex than that.

However, in the OT we clearly see new covenant promises speaking of a future, internal, and abiding work of the Holy Spirit in the lives of believers, most famously promised in Jeremiah 31:31 (Heb 8:8ff; cf. Ez 36:27), which speaks of God writing his law upon the hearts of his people in an intimate way. This "internal writing" promised in the Old Testament is the work of the Spirit. When we come to the NT, we read that the new covenant time is now. Jesus speaks of his blood as the pouring out of the new covenant for the forgiveness of sins (Lk 22:20; cf. 1 Cor 11:25), and Paul states that believers serve Jesus in the new covenant era empowered by the Spirit (1 Cor 3:3–18, esp. v. 6). What is "new" about the new covenant is not that OT believers didn't have the Spirit but that the people of God are now rightly to be considered a regenerate people. In the OT, there was a way of speaking about the people of God that often included the regenerate and the unregenerate; both participated in feasts, festivals, and worship gatherings. In the NT era—although any given church gathering has both regenerate and unregenerate people present—church membership, baptism, and communion are for the regenerate.

We should also note that some mystery remains about when we will experience the fullness of these new covenant promises. In some ways, they belong to the already-and-not-yet paradigm of so many other aspects of salvation and God's kingdom. We are saved, being saved, and will be saved; God's kingdom is come, is coming, and will come. So, with respect to the specific new covenant promises, yes, God writes his law upon our hearts by the Spirit so that obedience flows from the inside; but no, we are not in a time when we no longer need to say "Know the Lord" because we all know him (Jer 31:34; Heb 8:11)—not yet anyway. The best is yet to come.

Sometimes Christians are puzzled as to why it is advantageous for us, as Jesus said, that he go away and send the Holy Spirit (Jn 16:7). The ascension of Jesus and the sending of the Holy Spirit benefit us because God now dwells in every believer at once. Jesus, by taking on flesh, in his divinity remains omnipresent but in his humanity is henceforth in a single location. The Holy Spirit freely moves among us for our good—as he did to help Christ during his earthly ministry. We can't know definitively if Christ performed every miracle through the power of the Spirit as opposed to his own divinity, but Scripture often connects the two (Is 11:2; Mt 12:28; Lk 3:22; 4:1; 4:18-19; Rm 8:11; Heb 9:14).

The Holy Spirit is active in many things, but in "all that He does," he brings glory to Christ. One way he glorifies Christ is by convicting sinners of their sin and need for Jesus (Jn 16:8-11). Another way is by converting sinners, or regenerating their hearts as it is often called, so that sinners can put their faith in Jesus (Ez 36:25-27; Jn 3:3; Titus 3:5). Those whom the Spirit regenerates are graciously adopted into God's family (Rm 8:14-17). As in all the other aspects of redemption, each person of the Trinity is at work, but in adoption, there is a particular emphasis on the work of the Holy Spirit (Rm 8:15; Gal 4:6). Once adopted into the body of Christ, the Holy Spirit remains active in sanctification (Gal 5:22-23; 2 Thes 2:13), the process whereby believers become more and more like Jesus. Becoming more like Jesus, or walking in step with the Spirit (Gal 5:25), is one indication that someone who claims Christ is truly a believer. There are different aspects to the Spirit's role in sanctification, including the Spirit's indwelling, illuminating, guiding, equipping, and empowering. Indwelling is the Spirit's ever-present residence in the believer (Jn 14:17; Rm 8:11). Illuminating is the Spirit's enabling of the believer to understand God's Word (2 Cor 4:4-15; Eph 1:17-19). Guiding is the Spirit's directing of the believer's walk to glorify Christ (Rm 8:4; Gal 5:16). Equipping is the Spirit's supplying and cultivating gifts that the believer needs to follow Jesus (Rm 12:6-8; 1 Cor 7:7; 12:8-10, 28; Eph 4:11). And empowering is the Spirit's supplying of moment by moment power required to live for Christ (Acts 6:8; Eph 3:16).

This point in the book is probably as good of a place as any to state explicitly what has already been alluded to: my understanding of the order of salvation begins with the love of God, which leads to predestination and election, then internal, effectual calling and regeneration upon the hearing of the gospel (i.e., external call), which produces repentance and faith and our justification and adoption, which then begins sanctification, perseverance and preservation, and culminates in our glorification. Related to the order of salvation is the short but prevalent phrase "in Christ." Nearly one hundred times in the NT we read of believers being in Christ (e.g., 2 Cor 5:17; 1 Pet 5:14). Even more occurrences surface when we include variations of the phrase. In fact, sometimes the biblical authors even speak of Christ being in believers, not just believers being in Christ (Jn 15:4; Col 1:27). Union with/in Christ covers a range of aspects related to a believer's salvation. Simply put, to be in union with Christ is to have your life (now and into eternity) bound together with Christ in such a way that you receive all the saving benefits of the gospel (Col 3:3–4). To put it even more simply, union with Christ is like placing everything good about the gospel into a sack, labeling the sack "in Christ," and handing it to a believer.

It is important to understand the proper meaning of "baptism in/of the Holy Spirit" and "filling of the Holy Spirit." With only slight variation, the phrase baptism in/with the Holy Spirit occurs seven times in the NT (Mt 3:11; Mk 1:8; Lk 3:16; Jn 1:33; Acts 1:5; 11:16; 1 Cor 12:13). In the passages from the Gospels and Acts, baptism in the Holy Spirit indicates what Jesus commissions the Spirit to do in conversion, over and against the baptism performed by John: John baptized with water; Jesus baptizes with the Holy Spirit. That covers the first six occurrences, which leaves only 1 Corinthians 12:13. The meaning in 1 Corinthians is not immediately clear but is best understood as part of the initial process of conversion whereby believers are "baptized" into the body of Christ and drink down the benefits of being united to him. In this way, the passage speaks to the reality of adoption into God's family but does so using the immersion language of baptism—every Christian, whether ethnically Jewish or Gentile, gets fully dunked into the one body of God's family.

Variations of the phrase "filled with the Spirit" frequently occur (Acts 2:4; 4:8, 31; 6:3; 7:55; Eph 5:18) and carry the meaning of being under the Spirit's control or influence; being filled with the Spirit is a special empowering for service to Christ, which can include tongues but is certainly not limited to them (Lk 1:15ff, 41ff, 67; Acts 7:55). Being filled with the Spirit in increasing measure should be the healthy desire of all Christians. Lord, fill me with your Spirit to forgive an enemy . . . forsake my sin . . . fully trust your promises . . . and so on.

While the sign gifts of speaking in tongues, prophecy, and healing receive special spotlight in charismatic churches, this has not been my experience, and I am cautious about encouraging such expressions. However, I am not a cessationist, that is, one who understands all genuine expressions of sign gifts to have ceased with the closing of the NT canon and the death of the first generation of the early Christian church. I'm not convinced any verse clearly indicates the cessation of these gifts, and the plain reading of Scripture seems to suggest they haven't.

Another helpful distinction to parse is between the fruit of the Spirit and the gifts of the Spirit. It is clear from Galatians 5:22–23 that the Spirit produces fruit in all Christians ("love, joy, peace..."). As preachers often do, I'll note the fruit is singular but concatenated or linked. However, we should not expect all of the spiritual gifts to be present in every believer. There are five main passages in the NT where spiritual gifts, in the technical sense, are non-exhaustively listed (Rm 12:6–8; 1 Cor 12:8–10, 28; Eph 4:11; 1 Pet 4:10–11). A composite of these passages yields about a dozen spiritual gifts, including, but not limited to, leadership, healing, administration, teaching, mercy, and faith. I say "not limited to" not only because I didn't mention every gift listed in the classic spiritual gift passages, but also because we tend to leave off the other spiritual gifts mentioned in the Bible, such as the spiritual gift of craftsmanship mentioned in Exodus 31 and the gifts of singleness and marriage in 1 Corinthians 7:7. But however we round out the details of the list, the result should be thanksgiving among God's people because he so graciously blesses and gifts his church.

Discussion Questions

Person

1. Who is the Holy Spirit?

Purpose (in both the Old and New Testaments)

2. How is the ministry of the Holy Spirit similar and dissimilar between the old and new covenants?

3. Why did the Holy Spirit come, viz. why did Jesus send "another"? What does it mean that the Holy Spirit "glorifies the Lord Jesus Christ"?

Convicting the World

4. Why is the ministry of the Holy Spirit essential in the "world"? What is the guilt of which he convicts?

Regenerating Sinners

5. What is "regeneration"? Where in the order of salvation does regeneration occur?

6. How do you understand the teaching about the baptism of the Holy Spirit from 1 Cor 12:13? Regarding the Holy Spirit's ministry, what are the differences between baptism, indwelling, filling, and walking?

7. What does it mean that you are in "union with Christ"?

8. What is the meaning and significance of "adoption"?

Indwelling Believers

9. What are biblical evidences of the work of the Holy Spirit?

10. What role do the gifts of the Spirit play in the body of Christ? Is that role different today than during apostolic times?

11. How are the gifts of the Spirit and the fruit of the Spirit similar? How are they different? How do they function in your life?

THE CHURCH

7. We believe that the true church comprises all who have been justified by God's grace through faith alone in Christ alone. They are united by the Holy Spirit in the body of Christ, of which He is the Head. The true church is manifest in local churches, whose membership should be composed only of believers. The Lord Jesus mandated two ordinances, baptism and the Lord's Supper, which visibly and tangibly express the gospel. Though they are not the means of salvation, when celebrated by the church in genuine faith, these ordinances confirm and nourish the believer.

In the context of the Bible, justification is the legal declaration from God that he has declared a person "not guilty" and imputed Christ's righteousness to the repentant (Rm 3:21-30; 2 Cor 5:21). We call this exchange double imputation, the believer's sin reckoned to Christ and Christ's righteousness reckoned to us. All this good news comes by grace alone through faith alone in Christ alone. To say justification comes *by grace* is to say that the loving favor received from God is an undeserved gift (Eph 2:8; Titus 3:7). To say it comes *through faith* means that a person must look away from his own works and instead cling to and depend upon the provision of Christ (Phil 3:9). We add the word *alone* to grace to clarify that in justification we add nothing to grace or it wouldn't be grace; *alone* to faith because nothing more than faith is required; and *alone* to Christ because no salvation is found except in Christ. The reason we do not always have to say that we need faith *and* repentance, though the Bible sometimes but not always says repent and believe (Mk 1:15), is because of the proper understanding of what faith includes. Faith in Christ involves turning from treasuring *X, Y, and Z* to treasuring Christ, which must include repentance, the renouncing of our old ways to walk in obedience.

The true church is the sum total of all those justified by Jesus—throughout all time and place. We see this understanding of the church in Ephesians 5:25b where Paul describes the church as all those for whom Christ gave himself up. Jesus loves the church as a groom loves his bride. Jesus Christ is the head of every local church because he is the head of the true, or universal, church (Eph 1:22–23; 4:15–16; 5:23; Col 1:18; 2:19; Rev 1–3). As head, Jesus lovingly rules, commands, and nurtures his church, which is his body, and in turn, his church should respect and submit to his gracious rule.

A part of the church's role in respecting and submitting to God's gracious rule involves the practice of the two ordinances that Jesus instituted to be carried out under the auspices of local churches, namely, baptism and the Lord's Supper. I have experience in both paedo- and credo-views of baptism, and I see many strengths in each (as well as perhaps some weaknesses), but I do practice believer's baptism. Once a person has experienced the saving power of the gospel, we properly display what has happened on the inside with a sign on the outside (Rm 6:1–11). In this way, baptism parallels wearing a wedding ring. It signifies to the world that the person is in an exclusive relationship with another. The ring—and baptism—do not put a person in the special relationship; they symbolize it. At our church, we do not require baptism for membership, though we certainly encourage it and typically discuss baptism with those applying for membership.

Concerning the Lord's Supper, various views exist. The Roman Catholic Church errs in her sacramentalism, the understanding that sacraments such as the Lord's Supper (Eucharist) confer salvific grace to participants regardless of their heart posture. Although far less dangerous, I think the strict memorialist view goes too far in the other direction, as though all we are doing is remembering. Christians never *just* remember anything (cf. "remembering the poor" in Gal 2:10 means far more than recalling to one's mind that some people are, in fact, poor). When Christians remember the death of Christ by participating in the Lord's Supper, God supplies his church with nourishing grace and unites believers. In 1 Corinthians 11:17–34, all the negative observations about the church's malpractice of the Lord's Supper imply spiritual blessing when practiced rightly as together we "proclaim the Lord's death until he comes" (1 Cor 11:26; cf. 10:16). It's common to hear people say that the provocative "eat my flesh, drink my blood" saying of Jesus in John 6 points us to the Lord's Supper. But it's the Lord's Supper that points us to John 6! The bread we break and cup we drink is participating in Christ (1 Cor 10:16–17). In the Lord's Supper we taste and see that his body and blood are true spiritual food and drink.

There seems to be a biblical, gospel-logic order to these ordinances, namely, that gospel awakening should be shortly followed by baptism (Mt 28:19; Acts 8:35–39), which should be followed by regular participation in the Lord's Supper in a particular local church, all overseen by qualified shepherds. The last part of that sentence (in a church under the care of qualified pastor-elders-overseers) and the association in the Bible of the ordinances with whole-church unity (1 Cor 11:26) has implications on when and where the ordinances should be celebrated. A youth director should not baptize children while away at a camp, and four Christian guys on a hike or a small group Bible study should not hold a communion service. Even when the small group leader is a pastor-elder, his small group is not the local church but only part of a local church. (The inability of a shut-in to come to the regular gathering of the church isn't the same thing.) To be candid, our own local church could do a better job teaching about the ordinances. We noticed this last year when we changed the default method of handing out the communion elements. Rather than passing trays through pews, we began inviting Christians to come forward to receive, which showed us that a few unbaptized, young children were partaking as well as others we suspect have unclear professions of faith. Clearly, we have work to do.

Preamble

The Evangelical Free Church of America is an association of autonomous churches united around these theological convictions:

EFCA local churches are autonomous because no official, governing body higher than the local church (e.g., a bishop in Episcopalian government or General Assembly in Presbyterian government) decides matters of dispute, exercises church discipline, and calls pastors. Rather, each local church handles such things (Mt 18:15–17; 2 Cor 2:6). We recently updated our own local church constitution and bylaws, which were adopted long before I arrived. In one place, the document had said we were a *"completely* autonomous" church (emphasis added), to which I occasionally remarked in elders' meetings "there is no such thing." While each local church is in a sense autonomous, churches are interdependent, meaning we function best when we affiliate with other like-minded churches for the many benefits to each other and for the greater witness to Christ locally, regionally, nationally, and globally. Additionally, we too quickly forget that every church exists upon the faithful brothers and sisters who have come before us, even those who planted each of our current churches. Every church is a church plant.

There are different structures of congregational government, but each variation holds that the final authority, under Jesus Christ, belongs to the local church membership (Mt 18:18–20; 1 Cor 5:4–5). Membership in a local church is for believers, which is why the pastor-elders of our church listen to the testimony of every person applying for membership. Those reading this book who regularly listen to membership interviews likely know both the joys of listening to the redeemed of the Lord say so (Ps 107:2) but also the angst that comes when an applicant's testimony and gospel clarity are fuzzy.

In addition to being in the Bible, congregationalism has particular importance in the EFCA because of its European roots that reach back to the time shortly after the Reformation. The EFCA, although not officially organized and named as such until the 1950s, has strong ties to believers in Europe who sought the freedom to worship God without the constraints of state churches. Today the term *free* carries a different nuance in the EFCA, but the spirit of freedom continues in the way a local congregation rules its own body and decides on theological matters deemed to be of second- and third-order importance (Acts 6:1–6; 2 Cor 2:6). In our church this means membership must vote on matters such as amending the constitution and bylaws, calling and affirming pastor-elders, affirming deacons and deaconesses, approving the budget, and buying and selling property. A healthy church can thrive when each office—the office of pastor-elder, the office of deacon/deaconess, and the office of member—knows its role and humbly serves within it.

Discussion Questions

Justification

1. How do you understand "justification" (cf. Romans 3:21–26)?

God's Grace Through Faith Alone in Christ Alone

2. Define "grace" and "faith" and explain how grace and faith in Christ are related to justification.

3. What is the significance of the emphasis on "alone"?

Body of Christ, Jesus Christ as Head of Church

4. How are the scriptural metaphors of "the body of Christ," "the bride of Christ," and "the Head of the Church" to be understood?

True Church and Local Church

5. What is the relationship between the "true church" and the "local church"?

Local Church

6. What does it mean to be a "believers' church"? Why is membership important for a local church? What responsibilities do members have in a local church?

7. Address the various types of church government. What is the biblical defense of congregationalism?

8. Within congregationalism, how should the Pastor(s), Church Board (Elders and Deacons), and Congregation function together for effective church ministry?

9. What is your understanding of the statement that the "EFCA shall be an association and fellowship of autonomous but interdependent congregations of like faith and congregational government"? What does "autonomous but interdependent" mean? Why is denominational affiliation important for you and the congregation?

Ordinances

10. What is the meaning and purpose of baptism? What are the various modes of baptism?

11. What is the meaning and purpose of the Lord's Supper? What are the various ways this is understood?

12. How do baptism and the Lord's Supper relate to one another, i.e., is there a biblical order? How do they "confirm and nourish the believer"?

CHRISTIAN LIVING

8. We believe that God's justifying grace must not be separated from His sanctifying power and purpose. God commands us to love Him supremely and others sacrificially, and to live out our faith with care for one another, compassion toward the poor and justice for the oppressed. With God's Word, the Spirit's power, and fervent prayer in Christ's name, we are to combat the spiritual forces of evil. In obedience to Christ's commission, we are to make disciples among all people, always bearing witness to the gospel in word and deed.

Speaking in systematic theological terms, sanctification is the process of becoming more and more holy (Jn 17:17; Rm 6:11ff; Eph 2:10; 1 Thes 4:3; Heb 12:1). The Bible closely links "God's justifying grace" and "His sanctifying power" in this way: God's action of justification invariably leads to and produces sanctification, a cooperative endeavor by both God and the person. When God justifies a person, the process of change *must* begin (Jam 2:17–26). This change is not without setbacks, but one day, God will complete what he began (Phil 1:6). Hallelujah. The process of change varies in people: sometimes it seems nearly instantaneous in one specific area of life, and other times change plods along slowly, incrementally— two steps forward, one step back. The Lord surely has his reasons for the relative slowness and rapidity of sanctification, perhaps just fast enough so we trust he's still working but not so quick that we get cocky. With all of his riches, Jacob's limp wasn't a bad thing for him; it assuaged his swagger.

When we say, "live out our faith," we mean the deepening of a Christian's trust in the promises of God that leads to increasing, joyful obedience. We can call this "works," which is what Paul calls it in Ephesians 2:10. Faith alone saves, but the faith that saves never stays stagnant. In fact, Scripture is clear that final salvation requires good works—works produced by grace through faith but works nonetheless (Jn 5:28–29; Rm 8:12–14; Gal 5:21–24; 6:8–10; Heb 10:36; Jam 1:26; 1 Jn 1:7; and many, many others). To just highlight one aspect of our obedience, Christians should do good to everyone but especially those of the household of faith (Gal 6:10), which is not unlike the requirements for eldership which specify that if a person cannot care for his own household, something is wrong.

While all true believers are eternally secure, the feeling of assurance is not static. A believer's assurance to whether he or she is a genuine believer fluctuates for a host of reasons, and progress in sanctification is one of them. When a believer lives out her faith in humble, joyful obedience, she should be encouraged that she is indeed a believer and that all the promises in the gospel are hers. A Christian in overt disobedience—what the OT sometimes calls high-handed or defiant sins (Num 15:30)—might feel very assured of his own salvation, but we might better label his assurance as false assurance. John addresses the topic of assurance extensively in 1 John 3, in which there seem to be two related components: an ethical part of assurance related to a believer's obedience and a mystical, spiritual part that comes through the voice of the Spirit (esp. v. 24).

Jesus spoke of the greatest commandment as loving God and the second as loving our neighbor (Mt 22:37–39). We see this pattern reflected in the Decalogue (Ex 20; Dt 5). To love anything more than God, even good things such as one's family and ministry, involves elevating a good thing to the place of God, which is idolatry. Yet when we love God rightly and preeminently, we will also love the things he loves. And because God's own passions are committed to the poor and oppressed (Dt 10:18; Ps 140:12; Lk 4:18), the people of God ought to be characterized by these same passions—passions that translate to merciful gospel witness in both word and deed (Dt 15:11; Prov 31:8–9; Amos; Micah 6:8; Mt 23:23). In this way, each local church ought to be an oasis of compassion and an incubator of people zealous for justice as we extend the gospel and make disciples among all people, teaching them to observe all that Jesus commanded (Mt 28:19–20). I spend a significant amount of time discipling men who, Lord willing, will spend their lives discipling others into deeper understanding of what it means to follow God in the home, church, and world—that is, walking with God both when everyone is watching and when no one is watching.

We should not neglect the implications of the gospel's cosmic aim to restore all things, which includes social order, but neither should we conflate the proclamation of the gospel to simply doing good things. People changed by the gospel will do things like volunteer in a crisis pregnancy center and oppose local laws that might hurt the poor and minorities. Yet the gospel is not volunteering or lobbying, though it produces good works as a tree grows fruit.

Because God calls us to reach all people (1 Thes 3:12), ministry in general and churches in particular will always be messy. Sermons will be too long for some and too short for others. Worship music will be too expressive for some and too stuffy for others. Some will wrongly become dogmatic about secondary matters and squelch fragile unity and opportunities to build bridges. And that's all just within the church. With all these varying maturities, backgrounds, temperaments, races, ethnicities, and economic statuses, Christians reaching non-Christians will certainly also be messy. It was in the book of Acts. But diverse people rallying around the cross of Christ glorifies God in ways monolithic uniformity does not. For if God has seen fit to unite the two oft-opposed groups of Jew and Gentiles together in one body through the cross, then we should certainly seek the same sort of unity.

When speaking of various types of diversity, it is also helpful to point out what we don't mean. Sometimes when Christians speak of faith, we mean *the faith* as in an established body of doctrine (cf. 2 Thes 3:2 in the Greek, *hē pistis*). Jude wrote about "common salvation" and contending "for the faith that was once for all delivered to the saints" (v. 3). These phrases become meaningless if Christianity were infinitely malleable. Yes, the Christian faith has aspects of mystery, but the Christian faith cannot be all mystery lest there be nothing to call the Christian faith once-for-all-delivered.

In evangelism, discipleship, and the advancement of God's kingdom, there will always be opposition. Of this we are warned (Mt 10:16ff; 2 Tim 3:12; 1 Pet 5:8). Our ability to discern the exact makeup of the opposition—whether the world, flesh, or devil (1 Jn 2:15–18)—is often difficult. The categories mingle. Yet God has appointed means, or we might say weaponry, for service in the battle. These means are many and varied, but we can correctly subsume them under three larger categories: God's Word, the Spirit's power, and prayer in Christ's name, by which I mean prayer consistent with the will of Christ and prayed in his authority through our union with Christ (2 Cor 10:3–5; Eph 6:11; 2 Tim 4:7).

Discussion Questions

Relationship Between Justifying Grace and Sanctifying Power and Purpose

1. How do you understand the doctrine of sanctification? How is it related to justification?

2. What is the purpose and function of "works" in the life of the believer?

3. What is the relationship between a believer's sanctification and assurance?

Great Commandment

4. Why is love for God preeminent and why is this at the heart of understanding the Ten Commandments and is considered the first and greatest commandment of the whole of the Christian life? How does this relate to other gods and idolatry?

5. How does our preeminent love for God (and God's prior love of us) serve as the basis for our love for others? Is there an importance to this order?

Living Out Our Faith

6. Why is it important to distinguish between "the faith" understood as a body of truth and "faith" understood as the way in which one lives, viz. having been justified by faith, we live by faith?

7. Living out our faith begins with "the household of faith," which is evidenced in "care for one another." Why is this important?

8. What is the biblical teaching of "the poor" and "the oppressed"?

9. How do you understand the local church's responsibility and role in the world, particularly ministering with compassion and justice?

Combating Spiritual Forces of Evil

10. What is spiritual warfare? How should we combat the spiritual forces of evil?

Christ's Commission to Make Disciples

11. What is the importance of the command to "make disciples," and what are the God-ordained means of doing that?

12. The scope of this ministry is "all people." Support this biblically and explain the importance and practical outworking of this in the local church.

13. Why is it important to distinguish between the gospel and the entailments of the gospel? How does the gospel relate to deeds of mercy and compassion? What are the implications of equating them (e.g., the social gospel), and what are the implications of creating an absolute disjunction between them?

14. We are always to bear witness to the gospel in both proclamation ("in word") and in life ("in deed")? Give examples of how we can witness to the gospel "in deed."

CHRIST'S RETURN

9. We believe in the personal, bodily and glorious return of our Lord Jesus Christ. The coming of Christ, at a time known only to God, demands constant expectancy and, as our blessed hope, motivates the believer to godly living, sacrificial service and energetic mission.

Perhaps it would be helpful at this point to include a brief paragraph that is more memoir than theology. As long as I can remember, I have appreciated the EFCA; my family almost exclusively attended EFCA churches as I grew up, and my father often served as a lay elder. As such, in my limited understanding of eschatology, I identified with historic premillennialism. This view abided during my time at a conservative, evangelical Presbyterian seminary and continued into my first pastorate within a nondenominational, reformed baptist church. There, my fellow teaching pastors were both amillennial. By the way, I had tried to be hired in the EFCA directly after seminary, but at the time there was no room in the inn, at least very little room; I graduated from seminary on the heels of the economic recession and churches weren't hiring. But my hope was always to return to the EFCA. Then I did. Community EFCA in Harrisburg hired me. A year went by and, besides pastoring, I studied and refreshed the EFCA licensing paper I had written while in seminary. Still, my historic premillennial position abided. For those who were at my licensing council, you'll remember that what was otherwise a fairly smooth-going licensing exam, shall we say, had more than a few bumps when it came to the millennium and my allegedly questionable hermeneutic applied to the days of creation and modern day Israel. I wasn't lying when I said I held to historic premillennialism. But I was naïve—naïve not only about the influence of my seminary but also the influence of my fellow teaching pastors at my former church and my own hesitancies about some aspects of historic premillennialism. I'm thankful for those bumps, the pointed questions, and the one no-vote I received because together they sent me on a four-year trajectory to study the issues in more detail. I now hold to amillennialism, which, among other topics related to Christ's return, I will defend below.

Jesus will return personally and bodily (Mt 24:30; 26:64; Acts 1:11; Rev 1:7). This view stands over and against the view that a "return" of Christ in the hearts of his followers could fulfill scriptural promises. The two major interpretive decisions related to Christ's literal and physical return are the nature and timing of the tribulation and the millennium. With respect to the tribulation, many Christians interpret this term to refer to a period of intense struggle, calamity, and persecution or a "great tribulation," as Jesus calls it (Mt 24:21). Historic premillennialism understands the Bible to teach that the church, as a whole, will remain through this tribulation period and after a time (seven years being either literal or symbolic) Jesus will return to set up his millennial kingdom on earth. This understanding of the tribulation isn't too different from my amillennial understanding of the tribulation, though it obviously differs significantly on the millennium. Amillennialism rightly understood does not deny the existence of the millennium as atheism denies the existence of God; rather, amillennialism understands the Bible to speak of Christ's millennial reign to be taking place in heaven right now. The amillennial view is consistent with passages that intricately link the timing of Christ's return with the final judgment and eternal state (Rm 8:17–23; 2 Thes 1:5–10; 2 Pet 3:3–14), not two returns of Christ with a great intervening period of time between the returns, which would make for odd readings of passages like John 5:28–29 ("the hour is coming..." where the "hour" would be separated by 1,000 years). True, some passages in the OT, Isaiah 11 and 65 for example, seem to describe a time "better" than the church age but "not as great" as the new heavens and new earth. Yet these passages could be speaking poetically of the new heavens and new earth. In short, what some see as taking place in the millennium can actually be seen as taking place in the final state. A rigid interpretation of Isaiah 65:20, which speaks of those dying after a long life, is odd to me, when v. 19 speaks of no more weeping. How could physical death not produce weeping no matter how long one lives?

Additional consideration, of course, must be given to Revelation 20. I favor the interpretive scheme called progressive parallelism, which understands the book of Revelation to recapitulate similar sequences of events, often with each cycle moving the description of the end a bit further. So, for example, what happens with the seals in chapters 4–7 is roughly parallel with what happens with the trumpets in chapters 8–11, and so on. Space does not allow for much elaboration, but events like stars falling from the sky "as the fig tree sheds its winter fruit when shaken by a gale" (6:13) push me away from a more chronological reading of the book. Once stars have plopped upon the ground like over-ripe figs, there can't be much left.

Addressing the classic text of Revelation 20:1–6 directly, a few things should be said. A great case can be made for describing Satan as bound in the church age and unable to deceive the nations, at least to the degree he did in the OT (2 Kg 17:29; Mt 12:28–29; 28:18–20; Lk 4:6; 10:17–18; Jn 12:31–32; Acts 14:16; 17:30; 26:17–18; Col 2:15; 1 Jn 3:8). Also, the reign of God and Christ upon a throne is frequently (some say exclusively) spoken of in Revelation as taking place in heaven (1:4; 3:21; 4:5; 7:9ff; 8:3; 12:5; and dozens of others). The 1,000 years mentioned in vv. 3, 5, 6, and 7 from which all our millennial views build their name (pre-, -post, a-) could surely be, in such a highly symbolic book, a round number suggesting a long period of time (cf. the figurative use of 1,000 in passages such as Dt 7:9; 32:30; Josh 23:10; Jud 15:16; 1 Sam 18:7; 1 Chron 16:15; Job 9:3; Ps 50:11; 84:10; 90:4; Ecc 6:6; 7:8; SoS 4:4; Is 30:17; 2 Pet 3:8). And it doesn't feel like a stretch in context to see the "first resurrection" of those reigning with Christ as the believers raised to the intermediate state, whereas unbelievers do not experience this resurrection but only the "second death." Additional evidence for considering the "first resurrection" as those alive in the intermediate state (not those raised to life on earth during a premillennial reign of Christ) comes from the several parallels of Revelation 20:1–6 with 6:9–11 and the decidedly heavenly locale of those martyrs. The parallels are a little more explicit in the Greek but can still be seen in translations. Revelation 6:9 says, "(A) I saw . . . / (B) the souls of those who had been slain / (C) for the word of God and for the witness they had borne," and 20:4 says, "(A') I saw / (B') the souls of those who had been beheaded / (C') for the testimony of Jesus and for the word of God." Then add to this that the whole vision in Revelation 20 ("I saw," v. 1) feels very heavenly; missing from the text are earthly details about Christ reigning upon earth, the temple, the land of Canaan, and the holy city of Jerusalem (although perhaps some infer that the vision takes place on earth because the angel comes down from heaven). For all these reasons, I believe the amillennial view of a single, definitive return of Christ at the end of time cooperates best with the authorial intent of not only the broad witness of Scripture to the end times but the specific witness of Revelation 20.

Moving on, a theological tension appears concerning our expectancy of the Lord's return, but the tension is also seen within the Scriptures. On the one hand, many verses in the Bible seem to indicate that the Lord could return at any time and we must be ready for him (Mt 24:42–44; Lk 12:40; 1 Thes 5:2). On the other hand, many passages seem to indicate that certain events must precede the coming of the Lord, including the tribulation (Mk 13:7–8; Mt 24:15–22; Lk 21:20–30), preaching the gospel to the nations (Mt 24:14), signs in the heavens (Mt 24:29; Is 13:10), the salvation of Israel (Rm 9–11, esp. 11:1–2, 25–26), and the coming of the man of lawlessness (2 Thes 2:3). Some propose the solution of two returns of Christ: first, a "secret" or pre-tribulation return of Christ to rapture his church from the world before the tribulation and then yet another return to set up his millennial kingdom. This view is often associated with dispensationalism. The post-tribulation view, which I hold, teaches that it is possible that all of the signs have been fulfilled or could be fulfilled very quickly but that it is more probable that the signs are not yet fulfilled. Therefore, fidelity to God's promises in Scripture demands we maintain "constant expectancy" regarding Jesus's return, while at the same time make sure that when Jesus does come, he finds us not idle but busy at *his* work in *his* world in service to *him* (Mt 24:36–51; Rm 13:11–13; 1 Thes 5:1–11; Rev 3:3).

Concerning the relationship between ethnic, national Israel and the church, some go too far when they speak of replacement theology as though nothing special remains about the Jewish people and thus push them out of the way. A better term, it seems to me, is fulfillment theology because the OT hope was always for an expansion of light to the Gentiles under the reign of the Messiah, an expansion that did not push out ethnic Israel but instead reconciles them both to God in one body (Eph 2:11–22; Is 46:9). The true "Israel of God" was always a believing Israel, which today includes both believing Jews and believing Gentiles (Gal 6:15–16; cf. Rm 4:16ff). A passage like Romans 11:25–26 seems to expect an increase in conversions of ethnic Jews near the return of Christ, which is wonderful news.

On the one hand, no person knows the exact time of Christ's return (Mt 24:36–44; 1 Thes 5:1–3; 2 Pet 3:10; Rev 3:3), which should engender humility. On the other hand, while our interpretation of some specific aspects about the end times remains partially uncertain, believers in Christ must remain fully assured that Jesus will come. For those who have put their faith in him, it will be a glorious and joyful day—a reality that should propel believers "to godly living, sacrificial service and energetic mission" (cf. 2 Pet 3:14).

Discussion Questions

Personal, Bodily and Premillennial Return

1. Briefly describe your position on the second coming of Jesus Christ. Include your views on the tribulation, the rapture of the church, and the millennium.

2. How is your view different from other positions on the millennium? Please define the other positions.

3. Why is it essential to state explicitly that Christ's return is "personal" and "bodily"?

Israel and the Church

4. What is your understanding of the relationship between Israel and the Church as it pertains to eschatology? Comment on Rom 11:25–27.

5. How do you understand Jesus's teaching of the kingdom and how does the kingdom relate to eschatology?

Effect on the Believer

6. Why is it important to include a statement of humility regarding the exact time of Christ's return, viz. "at a time known only to God"?

7. How do you understand biblically "constant expectancy," and what does it mean to live this way? What is the importance of the word "demands"?

8. How do you define and understand the "blessed hope"? How does the biblical teaching of the Lord Jesus Christ's return bring you hope?

9. How does Christ's return motivate you "to godly living, sacrificial service and energetic mission"?

RESPONSE AND ETERNAL DESTINY

10. We believe that God commands everyone everywhere to believe the gospel by turning to Him in repentance and receiving the Lord Jesus Christ. We believe that God will raise the dead bodily and judge the world, assigning the unbeliever to condemnation and eternal conscious punishment and the believer to eternal blessedness and joy with the Lord in the new heaven and the new earth, to the praise of His glorious grace. Amen.

This next sentence is a mouthful, so take a deep breath. The gospel is the good news that Jesus, the long-awaited Messiah and heir of the Davidic monarchy, has come (Rm 1:1–5; 2 Tim 2:8), died, resurrected, ascended to his exalted throne, sits in heaven from whence he will come again to judge the living and the dead (Ps 110:2; Mk 12:36; 14:62; Acts 2:33–34; Eph 1:20; Heb 1:3, 13; 1 Tim 4:1), and by virtue of his atoning death and victorious resurrection, he graciously extends forgiveness, mercy, and righteousness to any and all persons who would come to God the Father through him in repentance and faith (Is 55:6–7; Lk 24:47; Acts 2:37–38; Rm 2:4; 3:22; 2 Cor 5:21; 1 Tim 1:16). To "receive Jesus as

Lord," as this article mentions (cf. Jn 1:12), means turning from our sins and trusting in Christ as Savior.

The gospel is both inclusive and exclusive at the same time. The gospel invites all people, no matter how wicked or vile, to experience grace (1 Tim 1:15). Whosoever wills may drink from the fountain. But God only appropriates the saving benefits of the gospel to those who place faith in Christ (Acts 4:12; 2 Thes 1:8). Ultimately many will persist in unbelief and so reject the saving benefits of the gospel. For them, an eternity of punishment in conscious torment awaits; this ought to grieve and motivate believers to manifold action. It is a sobering reality, repeatedly declared throughout the Bible and especially by the Lord Jesus himself, that hell is a place of unending torment in the full presence of God's wrath and away from his grace, love, and mercy (Mt 25:46; Lk 16:26; 2 Thes 1:8–9; Rev 14:11; 21:8; 22:14, 15).

The Bible does not often speak of the time between an individual's death and the final resurrection and judgment, or the *intermediate state* as theologians have often referred to it. However, the Bible is clear that believers will be in God's presence. After death, the souls of believers go at once into the presence of Christ (Lk 23:43) and await their reunification with their glorified bodies in the resurrection (2 Cor 5:6–9). Similarly, upon death the souls of unbelievers go at once into hell, awaiting the final resurrection where they too will be reunited with their bodies (Jn 5:28–29).

The Bible indicates differing levels of reward and punishment based on how a person lived with the knowledge of God that they had (Lk 12:42–48; 1 Cor 3:12–15; Jam 3:1). As has been discussed previously, the connection between receiving salvific grace through faith and the producing of good works is so strong that the Bible often describes the final judgment based upon works, as it does in the account of the great white throne judgment in Revelation 20:11–15 (cf. 2 Cor 5:10). In this passage, those who did not have their name in the book of life are judged for not having good works, while those who have their name in the book do have good works and are not thrown into the lake of fire. Related to hell and the lost, it is important to say two things that have not been stressed yet. First, unbelievers do not go to hell because they didn't know about Jesus; people go to hell because humans are condemned sinners, and hell is what sinners deserve (Rm 6:23; Gal 3:10). Second, as for those who have never heard of the gospel, we should go and tell them before they die so they may hear the gospel and might be saved. Now, it's common to hear stories of how God is pleased to reach unbelievers through visions, especially among highly unreached people groups, such as those within the 10/40 window, but these visions are only salvific if and when they connect a person to the content of the gospel, which must then be believed. In other words, there might be more people being reached than we are aware of, but clearly the ordinary plan of God is to send human missionaries (Rm 10:14–17).

Several passages in the Bible either imply or state explicitly that there will be a great renewal of the earth in its physical condition to make a suitable place for resurrected, glorified believers to worship God forever (Is 65:17; 66:22; Jn 14:2, 3; Rm 8:19–21; Heb 12:26–27; 2 Pet 3:13; Rev 21:1; 22:1–3). Since God is infinite, and glorified people will always remain finite, the new heavens and the new earth will be a place of unending and ever-increasing joy and happiness as God displays forever "the immeasurable riches of his grace in kindness toward us in Christ Jesus" (Eph 2:7). While we formerly identified with the man of dust, in the gospel we now identify with the man from heaven and all the glory therein (1 Cor 15:47–49).

"Amen. Come, Lord Jesus!" (Rev 22:20).

Discussion Questions

God Commands All to Believe the Gospel, Repenting and Receiving the Lord Jesus Christ

1. What is the gospel? Is the gospel a universal message?

2. What does it mean to "believe the gospel," viz. what is the importance of belief?

3. Define "repentance." What is the role of repentance in conversion?

4. What does it mean to "receive the Lord Jesus Christ"?

5. What is the importance of the universal command to believe, the exclusivity of believing the gospel of the Lord Jesus Christ and the eternal consequences grounded in one's response to Jesus?

Bodily Resurrection of the Dead and Judgment of All

6. What is the importance of the "bodily" resurrection of the dead (note Jesus's bodily resurrection and bodily return), and what does this teach us about humanity?

7. What is your understanding of the Judgment Seat of Christ and the Great White Throne Judgment of Revelation 20?

8. Will believers face future judgment? Explain the meaning of 2 Corinthians 5:10, cf. 1 Corinthians 3:12–15.

Unbeliever Condemned to Eternal Conscious Punishment

9. What is the destiny of unbelievers? What is the destiny of the unevangelized? What does it mean that unbelievers are condemned?

10. What is the nature of Hell, and does "eternal conscious punishment" mean?

Believer to Eternal Blessedness and Joy with the Lord

11. What happens to a believer who dies before the return of Christ?

12. How do you describe "heaven" and "life after death"?

New Heaven and New Earth

13. What is the relationship of the "new heaven and new earth" to the millennial Kingdom of Christ?

To the Praise of His Glorious Grace (Doxology)

14. Why is it fitting to conclude a doctrinal Statement of Faith with a worshipful (doxological) note?

PART III

PASTORAL
AND
PERSONAL
SECTION

CURRENT DOCTRINAL ISSUES

Marriage, Divorce, and Remarriage

God desires that Christians marry only other Christians. This follows from the prudent extension of 2 Corinthians 6:14–18 to marriage (cf. 1 Cor 7:39 "only in the Lord" and 1 Cor. 9:5 "a believing wife") and the OT passages about marrying those from other nations, which weren't so much about differing ethnicities or nationalities but religions (Dt 7:3–4; 1 Kg 11:1–8). It's a great evil to delegitimize interracial marriages, as some have done in the past and some continue to do in our own day. But based on these passages, I would not officiate the marriage of one person who professes faith and one who does not. Prudence also suggests that Christians enter the covenant of marriage only with Christians of similar conviction and maturity. The issues surrounding marriage of a previously divorced person are more complicated. The Bible presents two grounds for a divorce that *could* open up the possibility of a remarriage, namely, infidelity

(Mt 5:32; 19:8-9) and desertion (1 Cor 7:10-11). The ideal is always repentance, forgiveness, and reconciliation, but these are not always possible. Thus pastors must take into consideration situational specificity while at the same time giving serious weight to what Scripture teaches, especially God's hatred of divorce and the way the permanence of marriage portrays the permanence of God's love (Mal 2:16; Eph 5:21).

Because questions often arise about the definition of sexual immorality and desertion, allow me to discuss each briefly. I take Jesus's use of the word *porneia* (sexual immorality) in the exception clause in Matthew 5:32 and 19:9 to be a sort of "junk drawer" term incorporating many variations of sexual sin, especially when the specific word for adultery, *moichatai*, is used in close proximity (5:27 and 19:9). This is not to say I'd encourage a woman to divorce her husband because last year he infrequently and repentantly looked at pornography. In fact, I'd never lead with the encouragement to get divorced. But I am saying a spouse in habitual, intense, and unrepentant *porneia* might qualify. Through study of God's word and devoted prayer, I could very well imagine the pastor-elders of our church coming to the conclusion that a man who spent a decade at strip clubs and consuming internet pornography, even if he had not consummated an affair in sexual intercourse, could be divorced under the exception clause. Related to this, the desertion clause in 1 Corinthians 7 doesn't only mean a spouse has moved to Vegas without a forwarding address. There are probably multiple ways to desert your spouse. But saying, "He won't go shopping with me" or "She won't watch football with me," certainly do not constitute desertion. However, I consider habitual, unrepentant violence inflicted on one's spouse to be a form of desertion. We must hold strictly to God's commands, feeling the weight of Scripture far more than cultural trends. And it's wise for pastor-elders to have a clear understanding of how we define sexual immorality and desertion before cases of each arise. As a final comment, my discussion in this paragraph should not be understood as an attempt to create new categories for divorce but to give definition and application to what the two categories encompass.

Abortion, Infanticide, and Euthanasia

God values life (Gen 9:6) and takes no pleasure in death (Ez 18:32). Thus, so should his people. Because abortion and euthanasia are sins, our views of them transcend political party lines and our solutions for them will not merely be political ones. No individual Christian or local church can participate in every meaningful cause, but I do long and pray for more who labor to advance this biblical worldview so that it gives birth to life-affirming deeds.

Role Distinctions in the Church of Men and Women

God can, and does, give both men and women extraordinary gifts for ministry, but God has left the office of pastor-elder-overseer to men. Biblical support for this is seen in the following:

the responsibilities given by God to Adam before and after the fall (Gen 2–3; Rm 5:12ff);

the pattern of OT and NT spiritual leadership being placed mainly among men;

the parallels between male leadership in the church and the headship of men in the home as taught in places like Ephesians 5, Colossians 3, and Titus 2;

no explicit mention of women pastor-elders in the NT;

and, finally, specific passages like 1 Timothy 2:8–3:7 and Titus 1:5–9 which require male pastor-elders, something Paul even sees rooted in creation in the 1 Timothy passage.

At the same time, however, women can and should be encouraged to participate in significant Christian ministry.

Homosexual Belief and Conduct

Today, the church has a tremendous challenge but also opportunity when speaking about what the Bible teaches about sexuality. The challenge is to speak with humility and compassion and at the same time fidelity to the Word. Homosexual practice is against God's good design. It is a sin (Lev 18:22, 20:13; Rm 1:24–27; 1 Cor 6:9–11; 1 Tim 1:8–11), and must be called such (Is 5:20). However, alongside this truth, the church must do a better job of explaining the positive sexual design that God has established for society to flourish and winsomely invite people to participate in it.

Theology of Worship

All of life ought to be lived as worship (1 Cor 10:31), that is, living in obedient, glad esteem of the worthiness of God. It is appropriate that Christians gather regularly in local churches to both display and deepen their worship.

Speaking of the corporate gathering for worship, we endeavor to sings songs, preach sermons, and pray prayers that exalt what is true about God, faithful to Scripture, and celebrates the riches that are ours in the gospel. We seek to do all of this in an orderly way to build up the body with words intelligible to our people. The responsibility of leading corporate worship is so weighty to us that a few of us make time each Tuesday to debrief the previous week's sermon and worship service, always striving to improve our ability to rightly handle the word of truth, asking for forgiveness where we've failed to speak as well as we ought, and praying that our church would more and more fall in love with God and his word.

ISSUES RELATED TO LIFESTYLE

Spiritual Disciplines

God is pleased to supply his grace day by day and moment by moment to his people through spiritual disciplines. Therefore I actively pursue practices like evangelism, fellowship, prayer, service, and listening to the preached Word. I have my devotions in the morning before my family wakes up, attempting to read through the Bible cover to cover each year. As for prayer, I typically spend some time in prayer during my devotions. In conjunction with prayer, fasting—in both short and long durations—has been important to me.

Stewardship, Personal Finances, and Debt

God owns everything, yet he has entrusted humans with the care of creation (Ps 8; Heb 2); therefore, we should strive to be good stewards. The only debt my wife and I have is the mortgage on our house. We also intend to continue contributing to retirement funds. The Lord has been very gracious to us in these regards, and we feel blessed to extend God's money generously to our local church, as well as to other ministries and missionaries.

Sexual Purity

The Bible tells us, "Be holy, because I am holy" (1 Pet 1:16). There are certain temptations that tend to tempt men more acutely, and pastors and Christian leaders are not immune. As such, I will continue to seek God's help in regard to all areas related to personal holiness and trust Christ to give me continued victory and progress as I lean into the means he has appointed for such victory and progress. This is the heart behind the book I authored to help men struggle *against* porn, not *with* it.

Marriage and Family Priorities

God made it the duty of men to provide, protect, lead, and serve our families (Eph 5:22ff). It is not a role of entitlement but of sacrificial leadership. Thus, practically, Christ-like spiritual leadership in my home involves me being the one to initiate conflict resolution (as opposed to being passive), doing the dirty house-work jobs, providing financially, and, as needed, being the first to take responsibility and repent. God calls all men to embody these impulses, though the outworking will vary depending upon one's circumstances. May God supply the grace to do it with increasing success and joy. With respect to pastoring, my family is a priority above the church. This has many practical implications such as coming home around 4:30 every day, even if I go back out for an evening meeting, as well as cutting the occasional sermon illustration that might bless the church but not my children or wife.

Social Drinking of Alcohol

Alcohol was seen as a blessing by the Jewish people and a sign of covenant celebration of God's goodness and provision (Dt 14:26; Ps 104:15; Prov 3:7–10; Jn 2:1–12; Lk 22:20), but the use of alcohol in excess is strongly warned against throughout the Bible in both propositional statements and through sinful examples (Noah's drunkenness in Gen 9 and Lot's in Gen 19; Prov 20:1; Is 5:11; Gal 5:21; Eph 5:28; and many others).

In light of all these passages, I occasionally drink alcohol but always in moderation.

Accountability in Life and Ministry

There are several structures in place for personal and ministry accountability, including an engaged pastor-elder board and bi-weekly meetings with my best friend who asks hard questions.

ABOUT THE AUTHOR

Benjamin and his wife Brooke have six children. Benjamin enjoys reading, wrestling with his children, dating his wife, eating at Chipotle, and riding his bicycle in the early hours of the morning.

He earned a degree in mechanical engineering from the University of Missouri and a masters of divinity from Covenant Theological Seminary in St. Louis, Missouri. He is a teaching pastor at Community Evangelical Free Church in Harrisburg, PA. He is coauthor of *More People to Love*, *Enduring Grace*, and author of *Don't Just Send a Resume*, and *Struggle Against Porn*. He has also written for The Gospel Coalition, Desiring God, For The Church, 9Marks, and Christianity Today.

If you would like to read more from Benjamin Vrbicek, please subscribe to his blog, BenjaminVrbicek.com, where he writes a weekly post. You can also send him an email at Benjamin@fanandflame.com. He'd love to hear from you.

When God says, "Follow me," do you know how? If you work in Christian ministry, it's likely that at some point in your career God will call you from one church to another. Do you know how to make this transition effectively? Moving can be scary and full of questions: *Where do I start the job search process? Which people do I talk with, and what do I send to them? How do I know if my family and I will fit in at a new church?*

This book is intended to help you answer those questions so that the hiring process goes well. And when the hiring process does go well, a lot of pain can be avoided—for the pastor and the church.

To struggle *against* sexual sin is to be proactive. It means sounding the bugle and marshaling the troops. It means combating your sin, not being a passive victim. More importantly, to struggle against lust means you know there is something—indeed many things—worth fighting for. With 29 diagnostic tests for your head and heart, this book will help you fight the battle against porn.

Endorsements from Tim Challies, Tim Chester, Drew Dyck, Garrett Kell, and Jeremy Linneman.

93

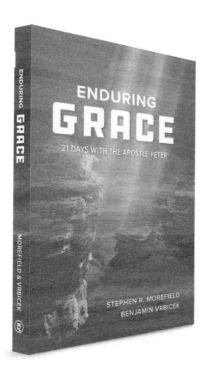

When tomorrow is harder than today, how will you endure? Peter preached boldly in one moment and cursed cowardly in another. His faith and obedience went up and down, down and up. But through it all, the grace of Jesus toward Peter endured. This is also how we will endure—through the amazing, enduring grace of God. Peter's story gives us hope that Jesus really is a friend of sinners and mighty to save.

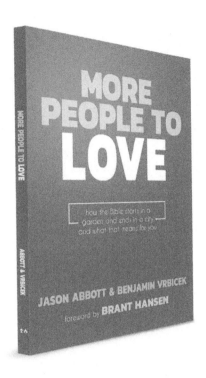

More People to Love **is about The Big Story of the Bible.** It's about God's plan, as revealed from Genesis to Revelation, to "make [his] name great among the nations" (Malachi 1:11). At times, our lives can be very difficult. But seeing our lives in light of The Big Story—the beautiful story of God's unfolding plan of redemption—gives us the perspective we need to carry on with joy and purpose.

Heb 13: ordination Message

Made in the USA
Columbia, SC
06 January 2020